Ireland:
Why Britain Must Get Out

CHATTO
CounterBlasts

Paul
FOOT

Ireland:
Why Britain
Must Get Out

Chatto & Windus
LONDON

Published in 1989 by
Chatto & Windus Ltd
30 Bedford Square
London WC1B 3SG

A CIP catalogue record for this book
is available from the British Library

ISBN 0 7011 3548 4

Photoset in Linotron Ehrhardt by
Rowland Phototypesetting Ltd
Bury St Edmunds, Suffolk
Printed in Great Britain by
Redwood Burn Ltd
Trowbridge, Wiltshire

Contents

Introduction

THERE IS a solution to the problem of Northern Ireland.

There is a way out of the endless cycle of killing and terror. It is for the British government to cut its connection with the state of Northern Ireland, and to get out of Ireland.

There is a strange conspiracy in Britain not to mention this solution. The government doesn't mention it; neither do any of the Opposition parties. The army hates it. The Press seldom discusses it. Television and radio behave as though they are bound by law not to refer to it.

In spite of the silence, one significant group continues to support the idea: the British people. Opinion pollsters are nervous of asking the simple question: should Britain clear out of Ireland?

When they do ask it, a majority of the British people answer, with increasing conviction, Yes. Why do the government, the opposition, the media and the armed forces so obdurately refuse even to recognise this growing and consistent majority?

They argue that the problems of Northern Ireland are caused by terrorism.

They say that there can be no solution to the problem until the 'terrorists are beaten'.

They assert that there is something particularly lunatic and fanatical about the people of Northern Ireland, and that no progress can be made until they come to their senses.

All this is nonsense. The problems of Northern Ireland are not caused by special flaws in human nature or by intractable divisions sent down to us by God.

They have human and political causes, which can be put right. Violence is not the cause of the problem in the north of Ireland. It is the result of it. Until the disease is treated, the symptoms will go on breaking out.

At the centre of the problem – and the disease – is the partition of Ireland nearly seventy years ago.

Partition: The Dismembered Corpse

IRELAND IS England's oldest colony. From earliest times it was a rich source of plunder for English kings and nobles.

Although Ireland was often invaded in earlier times, it wasn't finally conquered for England until the sixteenth century.

The method of conquest was to plant English and Scottish people in Ireland, and to grant them special privileges and rights over the land and native people there.

These English and Scottish people were Protestants. The native people of Ireland were Catholics.

The first problem was to transfer the land of the Catholics to the Protestants. The most effective way to do this was to kill Catholics.

The Governor of Carrickfergus in 1599 was Sir Arthur Chichester. He summed up the civilising mission of his first expedition into the hinterland as follows:

I burned all along the Lough within four miles of Dungannon and killed one hundred people, sparing none of what quality, age or sex so ever, besides many being burnt to death. We kill man, woman and child; horse, beast and whatsoever we find.

This attitude was taken up with enthusiasm by the Great Protector, Oliver Cromwell. He wanted the natives shifted out of the east coast of Ireland so that British people could more easily be planted there. He passed a law which condemned to death any native (or Catholic) who stayed on his land in the east coast. He showed he meant business by presiding over a massacre of Catholic people at Drogheda, for which he thanked God. If his policy had been carried out to the letter, some 80,000 people would have been killed. Fortunately for them the proposed victims saw sense, and most of them moved. In 1600, ninety per cent of the land in Ireland was owned by Catholics. In 1700, ninety per cent of the land in Ireland was owned by Protestants.

Terror was not the only method used to conquer Ireland. Sir Arthur Chichester warned, with characteristic sensitivity, in 1600:

It is famine and not the sword that must reduce this country to what is expected.

4

Famine was an extremely useful way of keeping the natives in order – especially in the nineteenth century. About one and a half million Irish people died of starvation in the potato famine of the middle of that century – a famine which was entirely unnecessary and was brought about by the greed and callousness of absentee British landlords, supported by their Irish agents.

To support three centuries of land seizure and enforced famine, the British devised the theory that the Irish were an inferior people. 'Ireland,' wrote the famous writer Thomas Carlyle, 'is like the half starved rat that crosses the path of the elephant. What must the elephant do? Squelch it – by heavens – squelch it!'

From time to time the harassed and usually starving majority in Ireland reacted against this squelching in the only way they could: by rebellion. Sometimes the spirit of rebellion infected even the Protestant people of the North. In the 1790s, as the effects of the French Revolution spread across Europe, talk of Irish independence from Britain became fashionable not only in the Catholic South and West but also among prominent Protestants in the North. 'England,' said Wolfe Tone, a leader of the 1798 rebellion, 'chokes our rising commerce at every turn'.

To counter this, the Orange Order was established in 1795. Its founding charter announced its main aim – which had nothing to do with religion. It was, it said, 'formed as a barrier to revolution and an obstacle to compromise.'

Its purpose, then and ever since, was to concentrate the minds and energies of the Protestant people of the North of Ireland on their religious superiority and to discourage them from any political activity which might weaken the connection between Ireland and England. So extreme and fanatical was the Orange Order in the years after the suppression of the Irish rebellion of 1798, that it was, in 1836, formally wound up at the request of the British Parliament and the British King. But as soon as both Parliament and King needed its organised support in Ireland once more, the Orange Order took the field again.

The Act of Union (1800) merged the Irish Parliament with the British one. This proved a convenient device to continue the plunder of Ireland all through the nineteenth century. Gradually, however, the demand for Irish independence from Britain began to filter through to the Irish representatives in the British Parliament. In the 1880s, for a brief period, a Liberal government depended for its majority over the Tories on the votes of Irish Nationalists in the House of Commons. This coincided miraculously with the conversion of the Liberal Leader, Gladstone, to Home Rule for Ireland. He introduced a bill into the Commons to grant independence to Ireland. Enough Whigs (Conservative Liberals) could be found to help the Tories defeat the measure.

The Tories had a card up their sleeve. Lord Randolph Churchill urged them to play the Orange Card. 'Let us hope,' he said, 'it will turn out the ace and not the two.' Ace it was, and no more was heard of Home Rule for twenty-five years.

In 1910, the Liberals once more relied for a Commons majority on the votes of the Irish Nationalists.

By now the Nationalists, under a landowner called John Redmond, were determined to win Home Rule for Ireland. The Liberal majority over the Tories was only two, and there were eighty-five Nationalists. The Irish MPs promised to support everything in the Liberal manifesto in exchange for Home Rule. The deal was done, and the Home Rule Bill published.

The Bill granted Home Rule to all Ireland. It was the will of the clear majority of the House of Commons.

The Conservative Party launched a ferocious campaign against it. They realised that some form of Home Rule for Ireland was inevitable. They sought therefore a means to hamstring Home Rule without defeating it. The means they chose was to play the Orange Card: to divide Ireland in two, securing part of the Protestant North for Britain,

7

while allowing the South a measure of independence.

The campaign was supported by rich and powerful people in Britain. There were two reasons for this.

The north-east of Ulster, where most of the Protestants lived, was rich. Belfast was one of the richest cities in the world. Its shipbuilding and its linen industry in particular could compete at a profit with competitors anywhere. These industries throve in the huge free trade area of the British Empire. Their owners and shareholders were appalled at the prospects of a new independent Ireland.

The dominance of Belfast and its environment over the Irish industrial scene was complete. Ninety-five per cent of Irish manufactured exports (including food and drink) were produced in Belfast. Nearly a third of Belfast's people (compared to only a tenth in Ireland's capital, Dublin) were employed in manufacturing industry.

To the greed of the shareholders in industry in Ireland was added the fear of the collapse of Empire. The British Empire was by far the largest economic unit in the world. If Ireland, the oldest colony, was to gain its independence as a result of nationalist agitation, what lasting hope was there of holding on to India, say, or Kenya or the Gold Coast or Malaya?

Edward Carson, a Dublin barrister, saw at once that the division of Ireland would deliver a death blow to the movement for independence. He summed up his approach in a single sentence:

If Ulster succeeds, Home Rule is dead.

The prospects, he foresaw, for an independent Ireland, restricted to the impoverished and largely agricultural South, were dismal. Shorn of its economic flagship, Belfast, and in pawn to the Roman Catholic Church, the new Ireland would be a laughing-stock – even a warning to any other country seeking independence from Empire.

These were the real reasons why men like Carson led the campaign for a divided Ireland. They were cloaked in the language of religion. What was in fact a defence of property and dividends was disguised as a defence of religious rights. Carson and his followers dressed themselves up as a New Moral Army, proclaiming: ULSTER WILL FIGHT AND ULSTER WILL BE RIGHT.

The Protestant people of north-east Ulster flocked to this banner with growing enthusiasm. The appeal for them was simple. They, the Protestants, were better than the Catholics. Many of them, especially the small farmers, might be poor. Their consolation was that they were not as poor as the Catholics. In an independent Ireland, with all thirty-six counties under one government, such privileges were no longer assured. The Protestants might have to give up their churches, their parades, their Boys' Brigades and all the paraphernalia of the Orange Order which regulated so many of their lives. This scare campaign blended exactly with the feelings of most Protestants. The Carson campaign managed in a few months to command the support of the vast majority of the Protestant people in the North.

That the inspiration for these people was that they should go on having it better than the Catholics, became clear in the debate which lasted from the beginning of 1912 and through the 1914–1918 war to 1922. The issue was the size of the proposed new Protestant state.

The first amendment which sought to exclude a part of Ireland from the Home Rule Bill was put down in 1912 by a Liberal backbencher called Agar-Roberts. His amendment suggested that four counties (Antrim, Down, Derry, Armagh) should be left out of the bill, and remain part of Britain.

Protestants were in a substantial majority in only two counties in all Ireland: Antrim and Down. They were in a slender majority in two other counties: Derry and Armagh. In the whole of the province of Ulster, which is nine counties, Protestants were in such a small majority that a slight shift in the birth or emigration rate could put the Catholics in the majority.

The slogan ULSTER WILL FIGHT AND ULSTER WILL BE RIGHT had therefore to be marginally adapted. It was no good pressing for a separate Ulster, which might at any time fall under Catholic control.

What about hiving off the two counties where the Protestants were in a big majority; or at least, as the Agar-Roberts amendment proposed, the four with a reasonable majority?

The Protestants were greedy. They were not content to live in an addition to Britain – an extra two counties attached, as it were, to the south-western tip of Scotland. They wanted their own *state*, with its own constitution, and its own government. Obviously, two counties were not enough to sustain a state. Nor, it was argued furiously by Carson and his Orange colleagues, were four.

Although nine counties was out of the question, the Agar-Roberts formula (four counties) was not good enough. Before long, the campaigners for a separate Northern Ireland had agreed among themselves that the best partition line would carve out Fermanagh and Tyrone for the northern state as well. In the interests of minority rights, the Catholic majorities of Fermanagh and Tyrone would be parcelled off into a Protestant state.

To the Irish Nationalist leaders, of course, the

notion of a divided Ireland came, initially, as a shock and an outrage. In April 1912, soon after the publication of the Agar-Roberts amendment, John Redmond said: 'The idea of two nations in Ireland is revolting and hateful. The idea of our agreeing to the partition of our nation is unthinkable.' At once, however, he began to think about it.

A year and a half later, on 14 November 1913, he was equally adamant: 'The exclusion of Ulster,' he said, 'would mean the nullification of our hopes and aspirations for the future – we will not be intimidated or bullied.' Almost as he spoke, however, he was being intimidated and bullied.

Joe Devlin, another Nationalist leader in the British House of Commons, exclaimed the next day: 'I would rather cut off my right hand than leave Ulster out.'

History does not relate whether Mr Devlin kept his right hand. But six months later, before the outbreak of the war, he and all the other Nationalist leaders, had agreed a deal with the Liberal government whereby the six counties of the north-east would be left out of the Home Rule Bill.

How did this extraordinary conversion come about? Initially, by the bullying and intimidation of which Redmond had warned.

The 'Free Ulster' campaign (though its aim was to free only part of Ulster) was not a gentle business of petitioning, persuading and appealing to reason.

Since there was no reason in it, it was based entirely on religious prejudice and discrimination.

Its central appeal was to violence. Carson and co. sent out a call to arms: an open invitation to defy the clear will of the parliamentary majority, if necessary by force. Carson mocked the government for not imprisoning him as he continued to campaign for a fight to the death against the parliamentary majority. He announced that he would break every law possible to achieve his aim. Bonar Law, the leader of the Tory Party, joined in the open defiance of parliament. 'There are,' he told a cheering crowd of a quarter of a million people at Blenheim Palace in 1913, 'things stronger than parliamentary majorities.'

Many army officers agreed. In 1913, a group of officers stationed at the Curragh signed a document making it clear that they would not take part in an attack by British troops on the increasingly well-armed Protestants in the north-east of Ireland.

Although the Prime Minister, Asquith, sacked the War Minister who apparently agreed to their demands, the Liberal government and its Irish Nationalist supporters were scared into submission by this great show of military strength.

Redmond, Devlin and Asquith reasoned like this. Half a loaf is better than no loaf. Twenty-six independent counties is better than no independent counties. It was better, they reasoned, to have two-thirds of Ireland independent than none of Ireland independent. Redmond, himself a landowner, measured the proposals in acres. Although he didn't want to lose the North, he was keen to gain the South. No doubt, he reckoned also that an almost all-Catholic South of Ireland might be rather easier to govern than an Ireland which included those troublesome and querulous Protestants in the North.

By 1914, then, the cynical deal was done. Ireland was to be divided.

During all the months of this tempestuous argument a lonely voice was raised against partition. The socialist republican James Connolly, the son of an impoverished carter in Edinburgh, saw at once what was proposed, and denounced it in a stream of brilliant invective which he published wherever he could. Many of his articles went into the *Irish Worker*, which had only a small circulation. Others were published in the Independent Labour Party Journal *Forward* which sold widely in the burgeoning British Labour and socialist movement.

James Connolly understood Northern Ireland from the point of view of a trade union organiser and socialist agitator. He had seen the effect of religious divisions on the working people, and he detested it. He noticed that while Belfast industry was making bigger profits than its equivalents in Liverpool or in Glasgow or in Manchester, the workers of Belfast were worse off. The Protestant workers did better than the Catholic workers, but both groups were worse off than other workers in similar industries in Britain who were not so obsessed with their religious differences.

To Connolly the division of Ireland on religious grounds was a nightmare. It would write religious bigotry and discrimination into the constitution. The two states would emerge not as republics but as helots to their churches. Let him speak for himself, since no political writer in our language ever expressed himself better:

> Belfast is bad enough as it is: what it would be like under such rule the wildest imagination cannot conceive. Filled with the belief that they were defeating the Imperial Government and the Nationalists combined, the Orangemen would have scant regard for the rights of the minority left at their mercy. *Forward*, March 21, 1914

> Let us remember that the Orange aristocracy now fighting for its supremacy in Ireland has at all times been based upon a denial of the common human rights of the Irish people; that the Orange Order was founded not to safeguard religious freedom, but to deny religious freedom, and that it raised this religious question not for the sake of any religion, but in order to use religious zeal in the interests of oppressive property rights of

rackrenting landlords and sweated capitalists. That the Irish people might be kept under and robbed whilst so sundered and divided, the Orange aristocracy went down to the lowest depths and out of the lowest pits of hell brought up the abominations of sectarian feuds to stir the passions of the ignorant mob. No crime was too brutal or cowardly; no lie too base; no slander too ghastly as long as they served to keep the democracy asunder.

Such a scheme as that agreed to by Redmond and Devlin, the betrayal of the national democracy of industrial Ulster, would mean a carnival of reaction both North and South, would set back the wheels of progress, would destroy the oncoming unity of the Irish Labour movement and paralyse all advanced movements whilst it endured.

Irish Worker, March 14, 1914

This passionate theme continued in article after article. It did not measure the proposed partition of Ireland in acres, as Redmond did, or in rows of pews, as the churches did. It measured the proposals by their effect on the Irish people. A Protestant state in the North would leave the Catholic minority *constitutionally* at the mercy of the Protestant Ascendancy. Coincidentally, the Orange state in the North would strengthen religious bigotry in the South.

The possibility of working together; of separating religious differences from political life; of winning advantages for all working people in Ireland – all this would be set back immeasurably by partition. Half a loaf with poison in it was not better than no loaf. It was worse than no loaf. It was better, Connolly argued, finally and logically, to go on fighting for independence for all Ireland than to accept the Redmond/Devlin/Asquith deal.

> I say that we would much rather see the Home Rule bill defeated than see it carried with Ulster or any part of Ulster left out.
> *Forward*, April 11, 1914.

James Connolly did not live to see his prophecy fulfilled. The Home Rule deal was postponed at the outbreak of war in August 1914. Connolly himself played a leading part in the Irish rebellion in Dublin at Easter, 1916, which was swiftly crushed, and its leaders (including Connolly) executed.

The rebellion unleashed precisely that agitation for which Connolly had hoped. In the elections held in Ireland in 1918 after the war, the old Nationalist party of Redmond and Devlin was annihilated. Seventy-five of the 105 Irish seats were won by the militant republican organisation Sinn Fein (Ourselves Alone), whose policy was to expel the British from all Ireland. Thirty-six of the new MPs were in prison. The South of Ireland was in a state of almost perpetual civil war. The British authorities, in particular the British courts, were hardly recognised. Sinn Fein set up their own courts and their own administrations, to which the people flocked.

It must have been clear even to the predominantly Conservative Cabinet in London (it was certainly clear to the Liberal Prime Minister, David Lloyd George) that British rule in most of Ireland was connected to a short fuse, and that the fuse had been lit. Rather than admit defeat and withdraw in as seemly a fashion as possible, the British government played the Orange Card. Their policy for the rest of 1918, for all of 1919, 1920 and half of 1921 was to hold down the South of Ireland by the most savage violence, while preparing to save the North for the Empire.

There was no attempt even to talk to the elected representatives of Ireland while this foul process continued. Mercenary troops without any sense of order or discipline were employed at high wages to ransack the South of Ireland, to murder its people and fire its cities. Meanwhile, the Government of Ireland Act was rushed through Parliament. It allowed for two Parliaments, both loyal to the British Empire, one in the North of Ireland, one in the South. The preparations went ahead for a new six-county state in the North; a state which was accurately described by its first Prime Minister,

Sir James Craig, as 'a Protestant state for a Protestant people'.

The entire British plan for Ireland depended on the creation of this new state. Carson's prophetic judgement was quoted again and again: 'If Ulster is left out, Home Rule is dead'. On June 23, 1921, the new parliament in the North was opened by the King. It had enormous powers. The British parliament stood almost entirely aloof. Although the new constitution contained a provision that there could and should be no discrimination by religion in the new state, there was no one to enforce the provision. It carried no legal force.

Two weeks later, with the Protestant Ascendancy safe and sound with its new parliament, the British government gave notice of a truce in the south. On July 8, 1921, the Sinn Fein leader, Eamon de Valera, came to London for secret talks with Lloyd George about independence for the larger part of what Connolly had called the 'dismembered corpse' of Ireland.

Negotiations about a treaty of independence started in October 1921, and went on until December. The Irish negotiating team included the IRA leader, Michael Collins, but not Eamon de Valera. Almost every detail was discussed interminably – the status of the new state in the Empire, the access to Irish ports of British ships of war, the oath of allegiance to the Crown, tariff barriers. None of these matters worried the British Ministers one jot. Their attitude was summed up by the Tory, Bonar Law: 'I would give the South anything or almost anything but I would not attempt to force anything on Ulster.' Bonar Law realised, as Carson realised, that once Ireland was divided, the property in the North was safe and the teeth of the movement against Imperial Rule were drawn. Any time the Carsons and Bonar Law had any trouble with the Irish in the future, they could play the Orange Card through the new Orange state which they had created in the North.

One by one, the issues were decided. Partition was left until last. One by one, like Redmond and Devlin before them, the Irish negotiators agreed to partition in exchange for a Boundary Commission which did not meet for two years and whose report was never published. It had never seemed to them a major issue. They, too, were measuring their achievement in acres, not in human beings.

On this issue, they were not out of step. When the Treaty was debated in the new Irish Parliament, the report took up 338 pages. Only nine of those were devoted to partition, and six of those to the speeches of the deputies from Monaghan which borders on the Six Counties.

The disagreements raged over many issues, but on partition there seemed to be general agreement. No one wanted the Protestants of the North in an independent Ireland. No one cared either for the half million Catholics who were permanently locked in a state which they had not chosen and in which they would be forever a persecuted minority.

In Downing Street, as the Treaty was signed, the Prime Minister and his staff opened a bottle of champagne. 'We gave almost nothing,' rejoiced the Cabinet Secretary, Tom Jones. The first colony had won Home Rule, but the wealth in the North was safe, and the newly independent people were enmeshed in a suicidal civil war. 'Divide and Rule' had been the slogan of the British Empire all over the world, and never was the slogan more cynically exploited or triumphantly vindicated than in the partition of Ireland. Sir James Craig, the new Prime Minister of Northern Ireland, came to Downing Street to join the celebrations. In a public statement, he said that any suggestion that people would be discriminated against because of their religion was a 'slur on Ulster'. He went on: 'A Protestant doctor has recently opened a Catholic bazaar, and Lady Craig has recently presided at a Catholic whist-drive.'

The Carnival of reaction was about to begin.

1922–68: The Carnival of Reaction

THE MAKING of the state in Northern Ireland was accompanied by what the *London Daily News* described as 'five weeks of ruthless persecution by boycott, fire, plunder and assault, culminating in a week's wholesale violence probably unmatched outside the area of Russian or Polish pogroms.' In that period, the entire Catholic population of the town of Lisburn were forced to flee their homes.

Almost all the Catholics who worked in Belfast shipyards and engineering works, together with the Protestants who were good enough trade unionists to defend them, were driven by force out of their jobs, never to return. In the years in which the state was born, 1920–22, fifty-three people were killed in Belfast in sectarian rioting; 11,000 Catholic workers were put out of their jobs not by their employers but by their fellow workers; 23,000 Catholics, more than a quarter of Belfast's entire Catholic adult population, were thrown out of their homes, many of which were burnt down. They crowded into ghettos, which rapidly became the only areas in the city in which they could feel even marginally safe.

All this violence was supported by the government, and by the new Northern Ireland Prime Minister, who made speeches supporting the actions of Protestant workers in clearing Catholics out of the workplaces. But the government and the businessmen who supported it soon became alarmed at the street violence. That violence remained as a permanent lurking menace. But what 'the boys' had achieved on the streets could now be achieved more easily and more lawfully by the government and the state which it set out to fashion in its own sectarian image.

The first problem was voting. The Government of Ireland Act passed by the British Parliament had insisted that voting for both Northern and Southern Parliaments should be by proportional representation. This could not of course subvert the permanent Protestant majority in the North. But it could ensure fair representation in the Parliament for the minority and was certain to result in Catholic-dominated councils in the Catholic areas, especially in the six counties' second city, Derry; and in Fermanagh and Tyrone.

Proportional representation also encouraged rifts in the Protestant vote. It enabled independent Labour Protestants to stand for election and get sizeable votes.

This was far too fair for the new Orange Parliament. In 1929, it abolished proportional representation, and reduced all voting to the 'first-past-the-post system'. In almost the same breath the new Protestant government set itself the complicated task of arranging the local councils to ensure that even where the population voted overwhelmingly for Catholic candidates, Protestant councils would emerge. The results of the abolition of proportional representation and the consequent 'gerrymander' (the fiddling of boundaries) were astonishing. In the 1920 elections, under P R, the Nationalists – who got the Catholic votes – were voted in control of twenty-five local councils (out of a total of eighty in the North of Ireland). Under the gerrymander, the Nationalists could win only two councils. The way the gerrymander worked in Derry, the second largest city in the North, was especially remarkable. There were 20,000 Catholic voters and 10,000 Protestant voters in the city. Almost all the Catholics were fitted into one ward, which elected eight councillors. The other two tiny wards elected twelve Protestants.

By this device the Protestant minority managed to control Derry council for nearly fifty years. In Fermanagh and Tyrone, both counties with Catholic majorities, the Nationalists lost the county council and every single rural council which they had won under P R. Even in the areas where they were in the majority (with one or two exceptions), the Catholics could not elect their own council.

There were further restrictions on the franchise. Only householders were allowed to vote, and businessmen got extra votes wherever they did business. This tipped the balance still more sharply against the minority. Thus, from the beginning, the Catholic minority were denied the central freedom of Parliamentary democracy: the right to vote out your council or your government. This was a parliamentary democracy which, because it had been set up in a sectarian state to be run by Protestants, could not deliver the most elementary right of a parliamentary democracy to a third of its population.

Naturally, the newly-elected councils and parliament, almost all with Protestant majorities, ensured that the few privileges which they could bestow were allocated exclusively to Protestants. If the majority were Catholics, they were allocated nothing.

Between 1921 and 1945, the Protestant-controlled Fermanagh County Council, despite the most desperate homelessness, built *no houses at all*. The guiding principle of all these councils was that, if council houses were allocated in large numbers to Roman Catholics, they would not emigrate. Instead they would stay, breed and perhaps one day constitute the majority. This may sound crude, but nothing was too crude for Protestant councillors when they were explaining the policy to themselves. One councillor, by name Tom Leevan, said in 1950:

> In Londonderry City and County, where we should have been on our guard, our majority has dropped from 12,000 to a perilously low figure. How did that come about? Through the ruinous and treacherous policy, pursued unwittingly perhaps, of handing over houses owned by Protestants to Roman Catholics.

Where houses *were* built, as in the South Ward of Derry, they were built in ghettos, in such a way that the estates could be effectively supervised or controlled by the police or the military. Over and over again the policy of discrimination divided the communities. Almost every wall became a wall of partition, another dividing line of discrimination and distrust.

The same walls went up in the schools. Indeed, the schools became the guidelines for the discrimination. 'What school did you go to?' was the inevitable question asked at every employer's interview. If the answer started with a Saint, so much the worse for the applicant's chances. The Catholic church cheerfully conspired to intensify the segregation in the schools. Once it had won the right to run its own schools, any complaints it may have had about the general policy of discrimination in education rapidly diminished.

At home, at school, and then on again to more segregation and discrimination in employment. Just as the best houses were kept for Protestants, so were the best jobs. As we have seen, even before the Northern state came into being, Catholics were expelled by force from the most secure of the Belfast workplaces. They never won their way back in any numbers to Harland and Wolff's shipyard or Shorts' aircraft factory or Mackies' or Musgraves' or Sirocco. In the civil service, whose alleged impartiality is the hallmark of Parliamentary democracies elsewhere, the appointments were made strictly from religious bias. The Prime Minister (who was made Lord Craigavon) set his own example. In a speech in 1934 he said: 'The appointments made by the government are made as far as we can possibly manage it, of loyal men and women . . .' (In the Orange vocabulary, loyal means Protestant.)

Lady Craig may have opened a Catholic whist-drive but heaven help any Catholic whist-player who dared apply for a job in her husband's civil service. Nor did the prejudice end at the civil service. For the Protestant leaders of the Protestant state, *all jobs*, however menial, were too good for Catholics. As in housing, employers were expected to show, above all, a sense of responsibility: a responsibility to discriminate.

Sir Basil Brooke, MP, was a junior Minister in the Northern Ireland government when he told a Unionist gathering in 1933:

> There were a great number of Protestants and Orangemen who employed Roman Catholics. He felt he could speak freely on the subject as he had not a Roman Catholic about his own place. He appreciated the great difficulty experienced by some of them in procuring suitable Protestant labour, but he would point out that Roman Catholics were endeavouring to get in everywhere. He would appeal to Loyalists therefore, wherever possible, to employ good Protestant lads and lassies.

In other countries founded on bigotry and discrimination the ban had hardly extended this far. Even in racialist South Africa it was considered reasonable for white people to employ black people in their houses. Nowhere in the world was bigotry taken quite to such extravagant lengths as it was in Northern Ireland.

The shape of the Northern Ireland labour force quickly responded to the distortions of discrimination. The traditional industries of the North were especially sensitive to the great slump of the 1930s. Thousands of workers in the North were thrown out of work. The total figures varied sharply with the rise and fall of the economy. The one consistent feature was that unemployment among Catholic workers was always double that of Protestant workers. Protestant unemployment was seldom higher than it was on the British mainland. It was places like Derry, Strabane, and Newry which consistently pushed Northern Ireland to the top of the British unemployment league.

The rigid policy of discrimination and oppression of the Catholic minority in Northern Ireland had, of course, to be carried out by force. It started, as we have seen, with the violence of the street gang and the riot.

But very quickly the Northern Ireland state voted itself powers to enforce its bigotry with its own 'law and order'. The newly enrolled Royal Ulster Constabulary, though many of its recruits were drawn from the Royal Irish Constabulary of the colonial years, was almost exclusively Protestant. Exact figures were never published, but the Catholic policeman was always the exception; the Catholic senior policeman almost unheard of. Nor was the Royal Ulster Constabulary expected to enforce law and order against the lawless minority on its own. In reserve, constantly on hand and patrolling, was the armed special constabulary: first the 'A' Specials; from time to time the 'C' Specials; but always the 'B' Specials, 10,000 men fully prepared for warfare. No one could be a 'B' Special who was not a Protestant. What remained of civil liberties – and there was very little – could be overturned at a stroke by invoking the Special Powers Act, which gave the government the right to impose curfews, to ban marches or demonstrations, to intern without trial – to do anything it pleased. The Special Powers Act was singled out for special praise by Dr Heinrik Verwoerd, racist dictator in South Africa in the 1960s.

So in the North of Ireland there were hundreds of thousands of people who were unrepresented in parliament or in the council, who were discriminated against in jobs, in education, and in social services, even highways and the collection of refuse. If they protested against any of these matters, or if they organised themselves in opposition, they were confronted by a 'law and order' dressed up in the uniform of oppression and bigotry. Discrimination infected every nook and crevice of the Six Counties. It dominated sport, which in itself was segregated. Catholics don't play for Linfield football club in Belfast. When an international Ireland player, Terry Cochrane, married a Roman Catholic, he was instantly transferred from Linfield. When another player came from Yugoslavia to boost the fortunes of Linfield, the fans cheered him to the echo – until they discovered that he had married a Roman Catholic. Then they booed, and he too was quickly transferred. Billy Sinclair, a former player-manager of Linfield, left in 1974 after getting engaged to a Catholic. He told me in 1984: 'If you're a Linfield scout and you see a lad who's good, the second or third question is "What school did you go to, son?" and if it's Saint something, then all of a sudden the boy isn't good enough. He kicks with the wrong foot.' These prejudices and discriminations have continued right up to 1989. They survived the passing of the Race Relations Act in Britain in 1965, reinforced in 1968.

When two Labour back-benchers suggested that the Race Relations Act, which made it illegal to discriminate against black people in Britain, might be applied to Northern Ireland where discrimination against Roman Catholics was part of the system, they were told that Northern Ireland politics were a matter exclusively for the Northern Ireland Parliament. It was not until 1976 that the British Government set up the Fair Employment Agency, with a staff of less than twenty, and with very limited powers to discourage discrimination in employment.

The most remarkable achievement of this backward, bigoted police state was its durability. Partly because of its isolation from British affairs, it lasted for fifty years with hardly a murmur of protest. The National Council of Civil Liberties sent a team to Northern Ireland in 1936. They concluded that under the shadow of the British constitution the Unionists had created a permanent machine of dictatorship. The word 'dictatorship' seemed a harsh one to describe a government which was elected regularly by its people, and which sustained a large number of elected councils. But the nature of the state itself negated that democracy. It made a mockery of the vote, of the opposition, of the civil service, of the police, of the media and eventually of the very idea that there was any democracy in the state at all.

In spite of the National Council of Civil Liberties' devastating report and conclusion, no one seemed to notice. Hardly anyone raised the matter in the House of Commons or outside. Neither during the 1930s, when many British people were sensitive to the growth of Fascism in Spain, Italy and Germany; nor in the 1940s, when the entire British nation went to war, ostensibly against Fascism; nor in the 1950s and 1960s, when legions were quick to demonstrate against discrimination in South Africa or in the Portuguese colonies of Angola and Mozambique, did anyone campaign against the discrimination which was operating in the most blatant and brutal fashion against half a million people who were separated from Britain by a narrow strip of water; whose government remained the responsibility of the British Home Secretary (though he never went there); and whose whole state structure depended on the presence of British troops.

The discrimination which disfigured the new Northern state also affected it economically. When the idea of the separate state first occurred to the British government, they imagined a contented and prosperous province which would pay its stipend to the British Empire. In fact the Northern Irish contribution to the Empire only lasted a few years. For three-quarters of its existence the state has not paid its way – but has relied on British subsidies.

As British subsidies increased in the 1950s, the enthusiasm of the British government for the Protestant state and for the Protestant people waned. The twenty-six county republic in the South of Ireland, though beset with difficulties, proved a more prosperous and profitable trading partner. In the United States of America, Britain's main military and economic ally, there were murmurs of discontent about bigotry and discrimination in the North.

In 1963, Terence O'Neill became Prime Minister of Northern Ireland. At once, the British government started to push him gently towards a rapprochement with the South. O'Neill obliged. In 1965 he met Sean Lemass, Prime Minister in the South of Ireland; he publicly turned up his patrician nose at the most boisterous antics of the Orange Lodge or the Apprentice Boys.

The backlash from the Protestants took both governments by surprise. For nearly fifty years Protestant people had been told that Northern Ireland was their state, and that they could do what they liked within it. They were told that Protestants were better than Catholics, and certainly deserved a better share of their state than Catholics did.

Suddenly a different tune was being hummed. To the new breed of ranters preaching the Protestant Supremacy the tune sounded like a betrayal. The Orange monster which, like Dr Frankenstein, Lloyd George and his Tory cabinet had proudly unleashed on the world, was not easily put to sleep. The Orange ranters bawled, and Prime Minister O'Neill crawled back into his Orange shell.

The next move came from an unexpected source: the half million beleaguered Catholic people of Northern Ireland themselves. For almost all the life of the Northern Parliament, these people had been cowed into submission.

In the turbulence after partition, many lost their homes; more lost their jobs. Their communities were besieged on all sides by armed police who represented a hostile religion and oppressive government. They were inclined to use their votes, but could see little point in it. When the Labour government in Britain abolished the restrictions of the local government franchise, which limited the vote to ratepayers and their wives, the Northern

Ireland government passed their own law. It maintained the restrictions on voting – and extended them. Ten thousand voters in Belfast lost their votes in 1946, because they were lodgers in ratepayers' houses.

Whenever the Catholics' representatives in Parliament tried to take their seats and play a serious role in the political process, they were met with cold contempt by the permanent Protestant majority. As they made their querulous complaints in a Parliament they could never control, Ministers turned their backs on them, read newspapers, smoked cigars. If they boycotted Parliament, as sometimes they were driven to do, Unionist contempt and laughter rose still higher.

From time to time sections of the minority resorted to weapons, and to the tiny remnant of the Irish Republican Army which had been cut to ribbons in the war of Independence and the civil war. But these old soldiers were out of touch with the new world, and cut off from their former sources of supply. Their few campaigns, as between 1956 and 1962, were disastrous.

The minority could not vote their way out of their distress; they could not sue their way out, since the law was almost entirely controlled by the Protestant machine; and they could not shoot their way out. No one in the world (least of all, it seemed, in Britain) took a blind bit of notice of them.

35

Suddenly the slow fuse which had been burning away in Northern Ireland for four decades ignited the explosive. The forgotten minority in Northern Ireland battered its way to the attention of the British government, the British people and the world outside.

1968–88: The Vampires
at the Feast

THE DAM burst in October 1968, when the newly
formed Civil Rights Association staged a protest
march in Derry. A similar march at Dungannon
the previous month had been blocked by police,
without incident. The marchers demanded an end
to gerrymandering and to the property restrictions
on the vote; a fair housing policy and a reversal
of discrimination in employment. These demands
were met with a ferocious police assault, which was
widely televised.

Suddenly the true nature of the police state in
Northern Ireland was exposed to the world. British
Ministers who, for fifty years, had not even acknowl-
edged that there was a problem in Northern Ireland
were called upon to do something about it.

What to do? The choice was stark. The first
option was perhaps the most obvious. The Labour
government in Britain, which had a huge majority
in the House of Commons, could have cut its links
with the Northern Irish state by announcing a date
for withdrawal and organising a constitutional conference to discuss the best means of laying the

discriminatory state to rest. No one in the government recommended such a course. It was not until 1971, when the Labour government was no longer in office, that Richard Crossman, who had been a senior Minister in Labour government and a close colleague of Labour Prime Minister Harold Wilson, advocated British withdrawal from Ireland.

Instead, the government in 1968 determined to deal with the problem by reforming the state, not ending it. The Home Secretary, James Callaghan, urged the Northern Ireland Prime Minister, Terence O'Neill, to proceed urgently with reforms.

O'Neill responded gingerly. The gerrymandered Derry Corporation was abolished and replaced by a Commission. There were proposals to end the company vote, and some of the worst aspects of the other gerrymandered local councils. But the demand – 'one man, one vote' – was not conceded. Extremist Protestant fury grew in protest against these very modest concessions. It quickly upset O'Neill's teetering support in the Unionist Party. He resigned in April 1969, muttering plaintively: 'If you treat Roman Catholics with due consideration and kindness, they will live like Protestants.' O'Neill was replaced by his cousin, James Chichester Clark, who had already expressed his distaste for one man, one vote, and who demanded from the British government more machinery for 'controlling' the rising civil rights movement. The Labour government refused. They continued with their policy of urging reforms on an increasingly reluctant Northern Ireland government.

In 1969, Protestant fury at the civil rights movement exploded in its traditional manner: attacks on Roman Catholics in the streets and in their homes. In August, nine people were killed and more than a hundred Catholic homes were burnt out in two nights of 'Loyalist' rioting, which was assisted with the guns and armoured cars of the police and the 'B' Specials.

The Labour government were forced to take the initiative – but once again the Ministers shrank from any decision which would end the cause of the trouble: the Northern state. They sent in troops which divided the warring communities. And they set up three inquiries: into the disturbances (under Lord Cameron); into the 1969 riots (under Lord Scarman); and into the Royal Ulster Constabulary (under Lord Hunt).

The Cameron Report uncovered the vast network of discrimination and bigotry which the Northern state had become. In round language, Lord Cameron and his colleagues declared that this was the main cause of the disturbances, and recommended a number of measures to end discrimination. The Hunt Report discovered that the

RUC was essentially a Protestant force. The Scarman Report blamed the 1969 disturbances four-square on Protestant extremists. The combined effect of the three reports was to ascribe the blame for the chaos in Northern Ireland to fifty years of discrimination and bigotry which pretty well no one in Britain had noticed.

Still the Labour government (and the Conservative government under Edward Heath which replaced it in June 1970) continued with the attempt to scotch the state, not kill it. Instead of withdrawing the troops, they sent reinforcements in the wake of the Protestant pogroms of August 1969. These troops appeared to most people in the Catholic areas as saviours: guarantors, perhaps, that the long night of the Protestant Supremacy was now over. But because the troops were sent in as servants of the Northern Ireland government they very quickly, and inevitably, became the servants of bigotry and discrimination. In July 1970, before a single shot had been fired by the IRA, British troops imposed a curfew in the Catholic Falls Road in Belfast – but there was no equivalent curfew in the Protestant Shankhill.

As Protestant fury rose, so the government in Northern Ireland was forced to back further and further away from the reforms which were pressed upon it by the British government. In March 1971, Chichester-Clark was forced to resign, and to hand over to Brian Faulkner, who earlier had resigned from the government in protest at its attempts to establish one man, one vote.

Any doubts among Nationalists and Republicans about the role of British troops were laid to rest in August 1971, when the army, against the advice of its own senior officers, carried out a ruthless policy of interning dissidents to the regime without trial. 365 people were interned, all of them Nationalists or Republicans. The operation was brutal and bungled. Several young men were tortured in events which later drew from the European Court of Human Rights the most savage denunciation of the British government. If there were any lingering doubts in Northern Ireland as to which side the British army was on, these were dispelled in blood in January 1972, when a routine demonstration of Republicans and Nationalists in Derry was attacked by British paratroops, who fired on the demonstrators, killing fourteen of them. Though an inquiry under the British Lord Chief Justice concluded unconvincingly that someone in the crowd had fired first, the central role of the British troops was now quite clear. If they had come in to stop the Protestants from carrying out their traditional pogroms in Belfast, they were now supporting the civil power in Belfast. The civil power was the old Orange monster, which was rapidly becoming more intolerant and more extreme.

In the summer of 1972, the British government finally lost patience with the Northern Ireland government, and declared direct rule from Westminster. William Whitelaw, a close friend of Prime Minister Heath, was declared the first ever Secretary of State for Northern Ireland. Again, however, instead of using its new power to put an end once and for all to the cause of the problems, the power of the Protestant Ascendancy and the state which bolstered it, the Heath government (with the support of all Opposition parties) made another effort to reform the unreformable.

They convened a conference at Sunningdale, Berkshire and proposed yet another form of government for Northern Ireland, one based on the concept of power sharing. The new government would consist of Ministers from each side of the religious divide. For the first time in the history of Northern Ireland, Catholics and Protestants would sit down together in government and legislate for the benefit of the whole community.

It was, undoubtedly, the boldest attempt ever to impose on the recalcitrant Protestant community in Northern Ireland some sense of fair government and equal rights. The new government took office on January 1, 1974. Its 'chief executive' was the Protestant Unionist, Brian Faulkner. Its deputy chief executive was Gerry Fitt, the leader of the opposition Social Democratic and Labour Party, which had inherited the old Nationalist vote and, with its new name, was making great efforts to change its sectarian image.

This triumphant initiative, supported to the hilt by the full might of the British government, all the Opposition parties and the overwhelming majority of the British people, *lasted five months*. In May 1974 (shortly after the Heath government had been replaced by another Labour government under Harold Wilson), an extremist Protestant organisation, the Ulster Workers' Council, called a strike. Its object was political: to bring down the government, to end power sharing and to restore to sole and exclusive power the Protestant Supremacy.

The strike lasted two weeks. At the end of May, the British government threw in its hand. The power-sharing executive resigned. Direct rule was restored. This was perhaps the shortest, sharpest and most successful political strike in all history. No attempt had been made by the British army to break it: there were plenty of signs that the army went out of its way not to intervene, in spite of clear orders from its political masters to the contrary. Harold Wilson was persuaded to cut from one of his own broadcasts a reference to the strike as a rebellion against the Crown. So, the entire initiative had been, like all the others before it, cast aside with a flick of the Orange wrist.

The six vital years between the civil rights explosion of 1968 and the collapse of the power-sharing executive in 1974 had about them a distinctive pattern. The British government's intention had been to change the Northern Ireland state by rooting out discrimination, gerrymandering and corruption. Instead the British government became the supporter, not the reformer of that discrimination and corruption. Its forces were the allies of the discriminators, not their enemies. The enemies of the British army became the victims of the discrimination: the Catholics, and in particular the Catholics at the bottom of the social scale who had, since 1969, been building up their own military strength to counter the attacks from Protestants and the British Army.

Since publicity is usually reserved for violence and murder done by the IRA, the figures make interesting reading. From 1969 to 1987, fifty-five civilians were killed by Republican or other Catholic paramilitary organisations; 601 by Protestant paramilitaries; 168 civilians were killed by British troops and the RUC. Sixteen of these died after being hit by plastic and rubber bullets, which were introduced because they were supposed not to kill. Between 1981 and 1987, 383 people were injured by these bullets. Many of these people were innocently walking the streets when they were hit. Dominic Marron of Belfast, for instance, is permanently paralysed after being hit by a plastic bullet. He was paid more than £100,000 compensation.

Recently the army and the police have readopted an old policy of raiding working-class Catholic areas, especially in Belfast. Whole estates are sealed off and suspect houses ransacked – often effectively smashed to pieces – in a search for weapons which rarely produces results.

Andrew and Janet Donnelly of the Turf Lodge estate in Belfast have had their fill of these raids. Their house had just been repaired from the last raid when the army and police launched a fresh assault in November 1988. (In that month alone, 700,000 vehicles were stopped and 1,100 homes searched.) When the soldiers came to the Donnellys' house they were equipped with pneumatic drills and electric saws. They tore down the kitchen which had just been fitted, and dug up the concrete floor, shattering a water-pipe. The Donnellys fled to a neighbour's house and took refuge while the soldiers tore up their house for thirty hours – taking time off for a nap in their beds.

Nothing was found. Eventually some compensation may be paid. But it is not hard to see why people like the Donnellys regard the British army as an army of occupation from which they need protection.

In spite of all this, however, all four Prime

Ministers since the troubles started – Harold Wilson, Edward Heath, James Callaghan and Margaret Thatcher – have insisted that they are 'reforming' the state of Northern Ireland.

Margaret Thatcher, for instance, signed a glossy pamphlet which was circulated to every household in Northern Ireland proclaiming her detestation of religious discrimination, and her resolve that Catholics would no longer find it more difficult than Protestants to get jobs.

How has this policy affected the Northern Ireland state? Certainly some *effort* has been made by the government agencies to roll back the tide of discrimination. The small Fair Employment Agency, set up in 1976, and armed with powers of legal enforcement, has harried employers to adopt a 'fair employment policy' towards Catholics. The Agency boasts some small successes. In Shorts aircraft factory, for instance, it claims that in 1988 Catholics formed eleven per cent of the workforce, compared to five per cent in 1980. But the agency admits that Shorts is an exception because it is regularly hiring new workers. In most workplaces in Northern Ireland, workers are being fired, not hired, and the old distortions persist. The percentage of Catholics in Harland and Wolff's, for instance, is less than five, the same as it was ten years ago. In their report for 1988, the Agency have a good word to say for 'new attitudes' adopted by another traditional Northern Ireland company, the cigarette company, Gallaher.

But the workforce in Gallaher factories in Belfast and Ballymena is still overwhelmingly Protestant. Only six per cent of workers are Catholics. Out of 200 skilled workers the number of Catholics is still nought. Moreover, the shape and powers of the FEA are strictly limited. Out of eighty-seven complaints in 1987–88, only three were upheld as discrimination and the average 'settlement' against a discriminating employer is about £1500. If an end to discrimination in employment depends on glossy pamphlets from Mrs Thatcher and the mighty efforts of the Fair Employment Agency mouse, there is no hope whatever for any marked change in the warped character of the Six Counties' workforce. The only chance would be a huge expansion of new jobs. Instead, jobs are being lost in Northern Ireland every year. Fewer people are at work in Northern Ireland now than ten years ago.

The unemployment statistics show that the gap between Catholic and Protestant has hardly closed at all since the British government became committed to reforming the state. In 1971, unemployment among Catholic males was 17.3 per cent; among non-Catholics, 6.6 per cent. The latest available broken down figures, those for 1984, show Catholic unemployment at 35 per cent; non-Catholic at 15 per cent. There is a faint sign that the size of the gap is closing, but the gap is so huge it obscures every other statistic. Protestant unemployment, moreover, has stuck fairly closely to the British average, while Catholic unemployment is nearly three times as high.

The new Northern Ireland Housing Executive has attempted to allocate houses according to need, rather than according to religion. This has meant a sharp change from the discrimination of former years. But even after twenty years of this relatively fair-minded executive, there is still a deep difference in the housing experience of the two religious groups: the Continuous Household Survey in 1983–84 showed sixteen per cent of Catholic households and six per cent of Protestant households with one or more bedrooms below standard.

The tiny steps forward against discrimination in jobs and in housing have been reversed by great lurches backwards for the Northern Ireland economy in the 1980s. Unemployment has doubled and the provision of public services such as council housing has consistently been cut back.

Discrimination at school goes on apace, and is sanctioned by the law. There are only two categories of people in Northern Ireland who are *allowed by law* to be hired on the basis of their religion – ministers of religion (which seems fair) and schoolteachers (which does not). Thus it is probable that in the enlightened 1980s *every single teacher* in primary and secondary education in Northern Ireland must have had allegiance to a particular religion before he or she got the job. This was every bit as much the responsibility of the Catholic church as of the Protestants.

What about the constitution? The British government has ruled directly in the North of Ireland since the ignominious collapse of the last Northern Ireland government in 1974. Save for a half-hearted attempt to set up another assembly in the early 1980s – the elections for which were boycotted by almost all non-Protestants – there has been no elected parliament at Stormont Castle.

The much-vaunted improvements in 1969 and 1970, therefore, whereby the electoral system shifted slowly towards 'one man, one vote', are of no consequence. There is little gained in having a fair voting system for a parliament which doesn't sit.

Voters in Northern Ireland elect seventeen MPs to the parliament at Westminster, one MP to the European Parliament, and local councils with very limited powers. The election of MPs to Westminster has little or no effect on the way Northern Ireland is administered. The chief interest in these elections is the swing between the conventional Nationalists/SDLP and Sinn Fein, the political arm of the IRA. As the IRA has grown in strength and influence, so Sinn Fein has won elections. It swept Fermanagh and Tyrone in 1981 when its candidate was the hunger striker Bobby Sands. Recently, it has twice (in 1983 and 1987) won a parliamentary seat in West Belfast.

But the Catholic minority are no nearer being able to vote their way out of their predicament than they were when direct rule was first imposed. They are as trapped as they ever were in the constitutional vice of Northern Ireland. They are, as ever, a permanent minority, utterly unable to make common cause with any other social force in their country, and so to get a whiff even of legislative power. Nor has the Anglo-Irish agreement, signed by the British Government and the Southern Irish government in 1985 without the consent or the approval of the majority in the North, made any substantial difference to their impotence.

The Protestant state for the Protestant people is every bit as sectarian as it was when it was first set up. Every attempt to reform it from within, whether by constitutional means or by political pressure, has been met with furious resistance, and has concluded in failure. For example, a cheer went up in the Catholic areas in 1970 when the Labour government in Britain finally agreed to disband the hated and sectarian 'B' Specials. Now the Specials have effectively been reincarnated in an even more offensive role. The Ulster Defence Regiment is an almost entirely Protestant regiment of the British

Army. It is recruited almost exclusively from the Protestant community; it is armed to the teeth by the British government. The Royal Ulster Constabulary is only marginally less Protestant than it was on the publication of the Hunt Report. It is still a profoundly sectarian force, with close links both with the UDR and with Protestant extremist groups.

The British government's policy for policing Northern Ireland has been, where possible, to Ulsterise. This has meant that the UDR and the armed RUC have been growing while British troops in Ulster have been (slightly) decreasing. In 1969, before they were disbanded, the 'B' Specials were 10,000 strong, and there were 3061 members of the Royal Ulster Constabulary. Today, there are no 'B' Specials; but there are over 10,000 members of the RUC, and nearly 3000 full time members of the UDR (and another 3364 part time). Roughly speaking, the same 13,000 Protestants are still armed.

The only consistent growth area in Northern Ireland economy is the policing of the minority by the majority. If you add ancillary workers and the prison service, there are nearly 30,000 workers in Northern Ireland – almost all of them Protestant – employed full time in the business of policing and imprisoning the minority. 'Law and Order' (Protestant law, Protestant order), is the biggest employer in Northern Ireland, and all the signs are that it will get bigger.

Far from cutting down the police in the police state it planned to reform, the British government has consistently strengthened it.

Perhaps the most profound achievement of government policy since the troops went into the streets of Belfast and Derry in 1969, has been the enormous increase in the strength of the IRA. In 1969, the IRA hardly existed. Its 1956–62 campaign had been such a disaster that it had effectively disbanded its units in the North. The Protestant pogroms of 1969 swiftly changed all that. As the British Army made it clear that its main enemy was the IRA, its main task to defeat not the violence of the oppressors but the violence of the oppressed, so new recruits from the beleaguered areas flocked to the IRA.

The chief result of all these years of containing terrorism, therefore, is that terrorism has increased. The IRA cannot defeat the combined strength of the UDR, the RUC and the British Army, which still has nearly 10,000 men in Ireland. It cannot win, but equally it cannot lose. So deep is its strength and support in the areas of Northern Ireland most grimly defaced by discrimination that it can sustain endless defeats, discoveries of its weapons, imprisonment of its cadres, and (worst of all) 'mistakes' in its terrorism, which have resulted in the killing and maiming of innocent people.

There is a stalemate in the North of Ireland. The Protestant state for the Protestant people is still there, nasty as ever, with all its partitions and bigotry. Its economy is, as two recent authors put it, a workhouse economy. Only nineteen per cent of the economy manufactures anything at all. The rest services and polices itself in an ever downward spiral of poverty, sectarianism and terror.

The British government (and the Opposition, and the media and the armed forces) all seem quite happy about this. They seem content that it should go on forever. There are some among them who say: 'Who cares? What difference does it make to us what goes on between two tribes somewhere over the water?'

It *does* make a difference to us – all the time. The chief impact it has on us is not the terrorism, terrifying though it may be; nor even the drain on the taxpayers' resources (the powers-that-be would probably find some other way to waste it if they weren't wasting it on troops in Northern Ireland).

The chief effect on us is the drain on our civil liberties. Bit by bit, the machinery of repression which the British government has constructed to save the sectarian state in Northern Ireland spreads its dark shadows over Britain. The Prevention of

Terrorism Act allowed any citizen to be held without charge, trial or explanation for seven days. From 1974–1987, 6430 people in Great Britain were detained in custody under the Act; 5586 of these (87%) were released without charge. From 1977–1986, 468,903 people were stopped and held for a while under the Act. In 1986 alone, 59,481 people were stopped – after which the government stopped publishing figures. This amounts to a vast infringement on the most fundamental liberties of thousands of citizens.

Almost every month comes news of more plans to cut down liberties to which we have long been accustomed: the right of silence for defendants, the right to a jury trial (most trials for 'terrorist offences' are heard by judges, sitting without juries), the right, whatever our views, to stand for election.

All these rights are either withdrawn or in peril in Northern Ireland. At the same time, the Security services get more and more confident that they can do what they like because they are fighting terrorism. The invidious and sinister march against liberties inevitably crosses the sea, and comes into our homes. Recently, the government arbitrarily banned the broadcasting authorities (but not the Press) from interviewing representatives of Sinn Fein, a party which returns an MP to Westminster and fifty-nine councillors. That ban applies *to us*. It stops us properly discussing what is going on in

Ireland. Before long, new measures will be foisted on us.

The argument will be the same. We must abandon the 'luxury' of liberty – to 'counter terrorism'.

It is impossible for us to go on curtailing other people's freedoms without eventually having to give them up ourselves. So the ugly, sectarian and violent stalemate which is set to continue in Northern Ireland will eventually lead all of us down the same path – into ugliness, sectarianism and violence.

All of this is quite unnecessary. All of it has come about because British governments since 1922 have not had the guts to admit that the partition of Ireland and the creation of the Orange state was a monstrous and cynical mistake, which must be put right.

Britain Out

MY PROPOSAL is very simple: the British government should declare that it intends to withdraw its troops from Ireland forever; and that it will no longer sustain a separate state in the North of Ireland. It should set an irrevocable date for that withdrawal, and at once convene a constitutional conference at international level to determine how best that withdrawal can be accomplished, and what contribution Britain should make to a new, united Ireland.

To this proposal there are four familiar objections.

1. 'We owe the people of Northern Ireland a duty. They have been promised again and again by consecutive British governments that their state will be sustained by Britain. How can we break these pledges to them without their agreement?'

It is quite true that successive British governments have made these promises. They are enshrined in the legislation which governs the North of Ireland, and in the recent Anglo-Irish agreement.

However, no promise made by a past government can bind a present or future government. If a government decides that the state which it set up and promised to sustain is no more than a breeding ground for religious prejudice and discrimination, it can and should break the promise to sustain it.

If there is a 'duty' to the majority in the North of Ireland, there is also a 'duty' to the minority. Even the original constitution of Northern Ireland demanded of the new state's government that it should not discriminate against the Catholics on religious grounds. This pledge has been consistently broken.

2. 'The Protestants are a majority, who have voted again and again to uphold the Northern Irish state. How can any democrat flout the will of the majority?'

The Unionists or Protestants of Northern Ireland have *not* always been the majority. The last elections held in all Ireland (in 1918) returned seventy-three Sinn Fein, six Nationalists, and twenty-two Unionists. The Unionists were then a minority. They had *always* been, in all Ireland, a minority. They were created into a majority by Lloyd George and his henchmen, who divided Ireland, precisely so that a majority could be made out of a minority.

Any minority which loses an election can always claim that, if the boundaries were changed, the election results could be made to look different. If a separate state had been created out of the city of Manchester after the British General Election of 1987, then Labour would have won the election there. The majority in the North of Ireland is not a true majority at all, but a cosseted minority which persuaded the British government, by defying the declared will of an elected parliament, to shift the goal-posts, and make it into a majority.

3. 'Well, if the Protestants of the North of Ireland are not a majority, they are certainly a large minority which fears, in a united Ireland, that its rights to worship and its individual freedoms will be trodden underfoot by a Catholic majority.'

There is certainly a deep fear of such persecution against Protestants in a united Ireland. This fear has hardly been allayed by the arrogant and offensive way in which the Catholic church, almost without opposition, has interfered in politics in the South. When James Connolly predicted that there would be a 'carnival of reaction' North and South if Ireland were divided, he was dreading not just black Ulster, a sectarian Protestant state in the North, but the untrammelled influence of the Catholic Church in the South. (Connolly was a Roman Catholic, though a bitter opponent of that church's interference in politics and in individual freedom.) His prediction has been fulfilled in the South as it has been in the North. Again and again the Catholic hierarchy has intervened to roll back progress in the South. The attitude of the Church to divorce, to abortion, to homosexuality and to a whole host of issues which affect individual choices is as backward in the South of Ireland as it is anywhere else in the world. Similarly, the progress towards a National Health Service and to a non-sectarian education policy has consistently been obstructed by a church which believes that health and education are matters not for human choice but of the ineluctable (and undebatable) law of God.

Protestant fears, therefore, have some force. But how best are minority rights protected in any society? Are they best protected by partition, by isolation of the minority in a separate state of their own? Throughout the world, where these problems of racial and religious minorities are repeated over and over again in a thousand different forms, separation and partition of communities on racial or religious lines merely inflames the differences, institutionalises them in politics and in government, and turns one former minority, fearful of persecution, into a persecuting majority, seeking others to discriminate against, to mock, bully and suppress.

Guarantees of religious and individual freedoms are what they say they are: *guarantees*, which every society owes to its minorities. The way to ensure that the Jewish or black minorities in Britain are safe from persecution is to hold out to them the rights of free citizenship which are available to everyone else; to ensure that there is no privilege afforded anyone because of their race or religion; and to persecute racial and religious persecutors.

Wherever such guarantees are upheld, they ensure freedom for religious and racial minorities a thousand times more effectively than do separate states which shore up the political power of gods or skin colour over human beings, and create and persecute other minorities.

4. 'If Britain pulls out of Ireland, there will be a bloodbath. The Protestants, all of them, will fight to the death rather than be part of a united Ireland.'

This is by far the most powerful of the arguments against British withdrawal from Northern Ireland. In support of it are called up the Ulster Covenant of 1912, and the undoubted determination in those days of almost all the Protestant people in the North to fight for their new state; the extraordinary solidarity of the Protestant people now against even the most minor move towards a united Ireland, such as the Anglo-Irish agreement; and the continued success of extremist Protestant ranters like the Reverend Ian Paisley. These are all signs, it is said, that the Protestants would fight with far more determination, unity and military skill than the Catholic minority has ever done. The terrorism of the IRA, it is said, would be as nothing compared to the violence which would be unleashed on the Protestant side if the British decided to withdraw.

It is a strong argument, which is often won because it is not answered. But there are many flaws in it.

The first is that the situation is very different to what it was in 1912 and 1922. Then, as we have seen, there were many wealthy and powerful British supporters of the Protestant cause. North-east Ulster was one of the richest places on earth, and there was a lot of money to be made by a lot of rich people if it stayed in the Imperial Free Trade Area. None of these arguments apply now. Northern Ireland is one of the poorest places in Europe. It suffers hugely from its isolation and its divisions. There is no reason, economic or otherwise, why anyone in the world should support a Protestant rebellion in favour of a sectarian and discriminatory state.

In 1912 and 1913 there was profound support and sympathy among the British people for the Protestant cause. A deep Imperial solidarity was tapped by the Tory Party in monster meetings and demonstrations. Today, there is very little such support. Outside the coteries of MI5 fanatics and military seminars, no one feels very strong sympathy for the Ulster Protestants. For every act of terror carried out by the IRA, there is another by a Protestant extremist organisation, and there is very little sign that people in Britain distinguish very carefully between the two.

The bedrock of British and international support, upon which the Protestant people could rest their case and from which they could draw money and arms in 1912, is no longer available to them.

What about their Protestant solidarity? Would they stand and fight together?

The existence of the Northern Irish state, and the support it gets from the British government and armed forces, is the central prop of Protestant solidarity.

One of the most significant developments of recent times in the North of Ireland is the fragmentation of the old Unionist monolith. This has shown itself, first, in the splits which have riven the Unionist Party – the splits to the right, which led to the Democratic Unionist Party under Ian Paisley, and to the left, which led to the formation of the small Alliance Party. Even more remarkable than the formal splits between the Unionist parties are the different views which emerge from every corner of Ulster Unionism about the best way forward for Northern Ireland Protestants. Some argue for the old order, the 'connection' with Britain; others for complete integration with Britain – another county of Scotland, perhaps; others for 'devolution' – a separate government like the old Stormont Parliament; others for outright independence from Britain. Fifty years ago, it was hard to find an Ulster Unionist who would speak ill of the British government, especially if it was a Tory government. Today in the North of Ireland there is among the Protestant people a profound opposition, rising in many places to hatred, to Mrs Thatcher's government. For all the froth and indignation which pours from the mouth of the Reverend Ian Paisley and his supporters, for all the huge crowds he still draws, the old Unionist monolith is split all ends up. A sudden shock, like the withdrawal of British troops, would open those splits up wide, and lead, among the Protestants, more to dissension than to unity.

The unity of the Protestant monolith in the past has depended on one factor above all others: the presence of British troops and the support of the British government. As long as the troops and the government from Britain are there to protect them, there is every reason for the Protestants to appear united. Their unity and their solidarity has been sustained for seventy years by the armed might of Britain.

Kick away that prop, remove British support for the Northern Ireland state and withdraw the troops – whom then will the Protestants be fighting?

Against whom will they be called upon to display their solidarity and their unity?

Separatist Protestants will be left suddenly high and dry without any armed protection for their state save what they themselves, without international support or sympathy, can provide. For the first time in history they will have to fight on their own.

It would be foolish to dispute that there may be numbers of Protestants who will be prepared to fight, and to unleash all the fury of four centuries on the neighbouring Catholic population, and on anyone else who comes to their defence. But the degree of involvement in such violence, the commitment to it, how widespread that commitment would be – all these are matters which are impossible to predict with any certainty. What must be likely is that the Protestant community would be far more divided and anxious as to their future than ever they have been in the past. Some would argue for an all-out war, which would almost certainly end in all-out defeat. Others would be unhappy about laying down their families' lives in such an uneven contest. Very few people sign up to die for their country if they know their country is going to lose. Even less do so if their country no longer exists.

The degree of violence, then, would depend very much on the way in which the withdrawal was accomplished. If there was any uncertainty or dithering in the withdrawal, this would fire the

Protestant enthusiasm for a battle. Moreover, any British troop withdrawal would have to be accompanied by a ruthless disarming of the sectarian elements which are currently armed by the British state. The UDR – the Protestant militia – would have to be disarmed. So would the Royal Ulster Constabulary. The slightest sign that the British government was still supporting the Protestant Supremacy would have to be removed once and for all.

The chief answer to the 'bloodbath' argument, however, does not depend on speculating on the likely balance of forces after a withdrawal. It rests on the *positive potential* on both sides of the border if the British troops are withdrawn. If carried out with a mixture of determination and compassion, there is every chance that such a withdrawal could break the log-jam of sectarian hatreds and suspicions which have plagued so much of Irish history; and could hold out a genuine alternative of free choice and free worship. There is a chance, after withdrawal, that Irish labour, so long truncated by religious feuds between workers, might come together to demand the new Ireland of which Connolly dreamed. In the shock of the sudden collapse of the Old Order, the positive sides of the people of Ireland of both religions could well prevail over the narrow superstitions which have kept them at each other's throats for so long.

Connolly warned of the vampires at the feast of the dismemberment of the corpse of Ireland. If the British connection is finally cut, if the two halves of the dismembered body are put together again, there is at least a hope that the carnival of reaction might be ended; and the vampires shooed away forever.

Is it really the case, after all, that Protestants and Catholics in Northern Ireland are doomed forever to hatred and strife? Do they disagree about everything, fight about everything? For all the gloomy history of that part of the world, there is plenty of evidence that when social issues become so large that they obscure religion, Protestant and Catholic people can unite. Whenever that happens, the people of Northern Ireland can suddenly become as strong and as confident as any other people in the world.

The rebellion of 1798, as we've seen, was led by Protestants. In the 1907 Belfast dock strike, in the campaigns against unemployment in the 1930s, even in the battle to save the National Health Service in 1988, religious differences have been shrugged aside, and the people of Belfast have forged themselves into a fighting force which seemed, momentarily, as if it could change their world.

It is on these occasions that the Orange and Green Drums have been banged most fervently, have shattered the fragile unity, and driven the two communities back into their laagers. The existence of the Orange state has made that relatively easy. The most powerful of all the arguments for ending the British state and for the withdrawal of British troops is that the impact of the change would remove the sanctuary of the Protestant laager, and encourage the more positive, optimistic and confident of the Protestant people to forge unity across the religious divide; to demand – and create – a carnival of peace, prosperity and progress, North and South.

Why, therefore, when it costs much more than it earns for Britain, when it leads all the time to the death of British troops and to the insecurity of British Ministers – *why* does the British government hang on limpet-like to the excrescence of the Orange state?

Some say it is for strategic reasons: that NATO bases in Ireland are crucial. This argument has little force. Britain left Cyprus nearly thirty years ago, and British bases have been sustained on that island all that time, in spite of the island's invasion by Turkey, and its enforced partition.

Some say that Northern Ireland is now an indispensable training ground for the security services; where the SAS can practise shooting people in the streets; where telephone-tappers, surveillance freaks, spooks and spies can carry out their sinister trade without check or accountability.

There is no doubt that the security services *are* free to roam at will in Northern Ireland, and many and fearful have been the results. Powerful though they are in the corridors of power, however, their operations are not reason enough on their own for Britain to stay in Northern Ireland.

The real reason can probably be found in the old rhyme of Hilaire Belloc:

Always keep a-hold of nurse
For fear of meeting something worse.

This 'something worse' might be the 'bloodbath' which so many people fear after withdrawal. In the past, British governments, after deciding to withdraw from colonies, have not been overly squeamish about bloodbaths. When Britain left India there was a bloodbath. When Britain left the Central African Federation there was a bloodbath. Yet no one but the most oddball reactionaries argued then (or argue now) that Britain should not have left these places.

The 'something worse', therefore, is probably not so much a possible bloodbath as the fear of a 'defeat'.

After each IRA bombing (on the whole Protestant bombings are not reported with the same indignation), the cry goes up: 'we must not give in to terrorism'. The argument is that the withdrawal of troops from Northern Ireland would be seen as a defeat for the British government by the terrorists of the IRA. Such an argument can survive in perpetuity. *Forever*, it can be argued, Britain must keep troops in Ireland for fear of appearing to be beaten by the IRA.

The best way, however, to defeat terrorism is to root out the cause of it.

The cause of IRA terrorism is not the moral degeneracy or otherwise of IRA members. It is the permanent persecution of a substantial minority who live in a state over which they can never have the slightest influence.

As long as that persecution – and that state – remain, terrorism, and the sectarianism which breeds it, are certain to continue.

The fear of 'defeat' therefore, is nothing more nor less than political paralysis. It conserves terrorism without ending it. It sustains sectarianism. It holds out no prospect of any solution – just another decade of hatred and slaughter; and another, and another.

It is time the British people shook their government out of its paralysis, by demanding that the troops come home. British governments and troops in Ireland have caused nothing but wretchedness and disorder for six centuries. Nothing would become them like the leaving it.

About the Author

PAUL FOOT was born in 1937. An award-winning journalist with the *Socialist Worker* and *The Daily Mirror,* he has also published several books – among them, *The Politics of Harold Wilson, The Rise of Enoch Powell, Why You Should Be a Socialist, Red Shelley, The Helen Smith Story* and *Murder at the Farm.*

CHATTO
CounterBlasts

Also available in bookshops now:-

No. 1 Jonathan Raban   **God, Man & Mrs Thatcher**
No. 3 John Lloyd   **A Rational Advance for the Labour Party**

Forthcoming Chatto CounterBlasts

No. 4 Fay Weldon   **Sackcloth and Ashes, or The World on the Brink of Success**
No. 5 Peter Fuller   **Left High and Dry**
No. 6 Mary Warnock   **Universities:** Knowing Our Minds
No. 7 Sue Townsend   **Mr Bevan's Dream**

CounterBlasts to be published in 1990 include:-

Tessa Blackstone on prisons and penal reform
Christopher Hitchens on the Monarchy
Margaret Drabble on property and mortgage tax relief
Ruth Rendell & Colin Ward on decentralising Britain
Ronald Dworkin on a Bill of Rights for Britain
Adam Mars-Jones on Venus Envy
Robert Skidelsky on British education and the GCSE
Marina Warner on children and the 80s

plus pamphlets from Michael Holroyd, Hanif Kureishi, Susannah Clapp and Michael Ignatieff

If you want to join in the debate, and if you want to know more about **CounterBlasts**, the writers and the issues, then write to:

Random House UK Ltd, Freepost 5066, Dept MH, London WC1B 3BR